MW00929915

THE FUNNIEST BABY NAME BOOK IN AMERICA!

The "Other" Book OF BABY NAMES

You named me what?

by R. U. Kidding

Go to: www.otherbookofbabynames.com

ISBN: 1456303619
ISBN-13: 9781456303617
LCCN: 2010916014

ACKNOWLEDGMENTS

In memory of my mother, Josie, a real writer.

Dedicated to my wife, Sassy, and my children, Bobbyv, Latesha, and Miguelito.

Special thanks to Anfernee, Patty La, Lynnessee, Baby Josie, Johnny W., Gerald Anthony, DDP, Coach "D", and to all of my friends and family who contributed names, advice and encouragement.

TABLE OF CONTENTS

INTRODUCTION

If you are looking for a traditional book of baby names, you probably should put this book back on the shelf. This is The "OTHER" Book of Baby Names! A collection of real names, or should I say, really unusual names, over 20 years in the making. I can assure you that this book will leave you laughing, and wondering why in the world some parents would saddle their offspring with these names.

I know that we live in a time where we all are frantic to ensure that our children feel SPECIAL* and UNIQUE*, but these folks have taken it to a whole new level. After reading this book you may feel overwhelmed. These parents have been so creative in selecting their children's names that you may not think you can measure up. All I can tell you is, don't worry. You can be just as creative! All you need to do is to take a traditional name, drop a few letters, add a hyphen or an apostrophe, a "sha" or a "la", and a well placed accent mark, and your baby's name stands a good chance of being in my next book.

Or perhaps you will want to borrow a word not commonly associated with a human being's name, like some of these parents did. Just open a medical dictionary or your refrigerator and your choices will be limitless! There are plenty of bodily functions and condiments that probably have not yet been seen on a birth certificate.

Of course, you can always use one of the names in this book. There are many to choose from. Your child will still be different. Trust me on this. However, I caution you that one day your baby girl or boy will grow up, and then, well, you know what they say about payback.

The "OTHER" Book of Baby Names is one of a kind. There is not another book like it in existence. In that respect, it is just like most of the names that you are going to read about. This book is broken down into chapters with titles like "Medical", "Royalty", "Household Items", "Clever Matches", and "We Need More Apostrophes". There are over 500 names. Most of the names come with a comment or definition. Feel free to select any one or more of these names for your poor, defenseless child. It's almost guaranteed that they will be the only one in their school with the name. Just make sure they know how to spell it before school begins!

1

All of the names contained in The "Other" Book of Baby Names have been personally gathered and verified by the author. I started gathering the names that make up this book in 1986. The overwhelming majority of names have been provided to me by my colleagues, family and friends from Pennsylvania, Maryland, Illinois, Virginia, California, New York, Ohio, Florida, and Iowa. Many were obtained from local and national newspapers, and television.

Whenever a name was particularly outrageous, or just too crazy to believe that it was real (this describes many of the names), written verification of the name was required. Many of the names were verified through the national White Pages online directory. I have first-hand knowledge of every name. These are actual names of real people! There are no urban legend names, like no'smoking and female' in this book (although they may be real). All of these names belong to people who are United States citizens, born and raised in the US. Although most of these names might be foreign to you (if they're not, you need help!), they are not names belonging to foreign people or their offspring. So, these people have no excuses for what they've done. These are your fellow Americans in all of their glory, determined to leave their mark on the world through their child's name.

This book will make a great gift for any mommy or daddy-to-be. Baby showers will never be the same, nor more fun, once this book starts to make its way around the room. Please visit our interactive website: "theotherbookofbabynames.com" and register for our Name Of the Day. Tell us about your particular favorite name from the book, or a name that isn't in the book that you would like to share with us.

I hope you have an opportunity to enjoy this book with your family and friends like I have been doing for many years. As my list of names kept expanding and was passed around the country, I often heard, "You should write a book!" Well here it is. It's good clean fun at someone else's expense. What could be better than that!

ENJOY!!
*actual names

1

THERE OUGHT TO BE A TEST

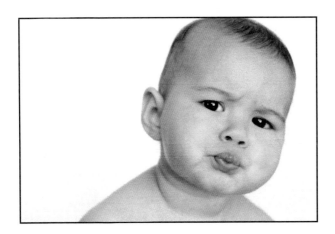

If you're like me you've probably thought on more than one occasion that there ought to be a test that prospective parents should have to take before being allowed to procreate. If you think this statement is a bit harsh, I'd ask you to be honest with yourself for just a moment. When you see a 3-year-old boy sporting a mullet, with a rat tail and a pierced ear, tell me that this thought didn't cross your mind, for at least a second.

It wouldn't be a very difficult test, nor would it be lengthy. It would simply be a way to assure that people possess the essential basics to raise their children. Here are some questions that I would suggest be included in the exam. Please feel free to add your own.

1)   **Select the item that is not appropriate for a child?**

   a)   A good education
   b)   Nutritious food
   c)   A clean and safe home
   d)   Internet porn

2)   **Do you think that grape soda is a substitute breakfast drink for orange juice?**

3)   **How many piercings are appropriate for your daughter before age 5?**

   a)   One
   b)   Five
   c)   Ten

4)   **What age is appropriate for your son to wear a Hooters t-shirt?**

   a)   One
   b)   Five
   c)   Twenty-one
   d)   Doesn't that come in the going home bag from the hospital?

5)   **1+1 = ?**

6)   **How long should you leave your kids in the car while you have some beers with your buddies at the corner tavern?**

7)   **Would you name your child after fecal matter? (fecal matter means poop)**

8) Has anyone ever told you that you, "don't have a lick of common sense"?

9) Do you jump to your feet and pump your fist whenever you hear the song "Harper Valley PTA"?

10) Choose two foods that are healthy for children:

    a) Doritos (Original)
    b) Nacho Doritos
    c) Ranch Doritos
    d) Broccoli
    e) Mountain Dew
    f) Carrots

Let me know how you think these kids' parents would have faired on the test. By the way, for those of you that may need some help completing the test, the answer key is in the back of the book. (jk)

TOP NAMES

PRECOCIOUS *(Pro: Pre-ko-shis)*

This is what you name your daughter when you want to be a grandmother before age 35.

MARIJUANA *(Pro: mar-uh-wah-nuh)*

Wonder what mom was doing before she got knocked up.

ROTUNDA *(Pro: Ro-tun-duh)*

Have mercy on her parents for they know not what they do.

DELETA *(Pro: de le ta)*

Let's take up a collection to erase her parents.

BEHAVIOR *(Pro: be-heyv-yer)*

Naming your child "Behavior" is a textbook example of bad Behavior.

LYNCHISTILIA *(Pro: linch-i-still-ya)*

Have these people lost their freakin' minds? They had better hope that there are no ropes lying around.

ABOUT *(Pro: uh-bout)*

What "About" this name? It's just a suggestion, but I'd take a pass on this one if I were you.

CAPRICIOUS *(Pro: kuh-prish-uhsh)*

They were going to name her Jennifer, but had a sudden change of mind without any apparent or adequate reason.

KARIZMA *(Pro: kuh-riz-muh)*

I'm thinking that maybe there should be a test to see if some prospective parents are even qualified to take the prospective parent test!

NAKEDRIA *(Pro: na-ked'-ri-a)*

A note to Mom and Dad. Your daughter's name has the word NAKED in it!

ASSHOLE *(Pro: a-sole-lay)*

Mom must have been one of these, for real.

DEJOIR *(Pro: de-jur)*

Guess what this child's nickname will be? "Soup," of course.

SAMARIUM *(Pro: suh-mar-ee-um)*

I'm assuming you are all familiar with the story of the Good Samarium.

ANJOYLUS   *(Pro: ann-joy-les)*

Any name that incorporates a word that means giving no pleasure or gladness cannot possibly have a positive impact on the lucky recipient.

KAWANIS   *(Pro: Ka-wa-nis)*

A great service organization that would probably never extend a membership invitation to the father of this child despite the free publicity.

PERIJAH   *(Pro: puh-rye-uh)*

Tyra = Nice name
Mariah = Beautiful name
Perijah = "If you want other children to run away from your child" name

SHITTHEAD   *(Pro: Shi-theed)*

Def: Fecal matter head
I'm sad to report that despite my best efforts to debunk this name as being an actual name, I failed miserably. This name is real! I feel like a real Shitthead for doubting my source. Please join me in saying a prayer for this child.

SHYREEKA   *(Pro: shy-reek-a)*

I must be losing my mind. Did these morons really name their daughter Shyreeka

2

AUTOMOTIVE DEPARTMENT

Americans are car crazy. More than just a means of transportation, our motor vehicles have become a reflection of our lifestyle, values, who we think we are, and who we think we want to be. Apparently, some of us are so in love with our automobiles that we decided to name our children after our favorite car. Why would some parents indulge themselves in this manner? I can't really answer that question as I do not have a psychology degree. However, I do feel safe in saying that these parents are probably the same people that will pull up next to you in a 20 year old beater, with one window covered with plastic, a rear bumper held up with duct tape, and then floor it to get the jump on you!

TOP NAMES

PORSCHE *(Pro: poor-shuh ~ or ~ poor-shhh)*

A German sports car, known for its speed, road handling ability, and rear engine position.

This young lady probably doesn't even know what a Porsche is. In any event, for her sake, I hope she doesn't become known for her speed, handling ability, and rear engine position.

Spinoff Names: Porsha, Laporsha, Japorsha, Portia

A LEXUS *(Pro: uh-lex-us)*

Lexus is a Japanese manufacturer of automobiles known for their quality and dependability.

I'm going out on a limb here, but I'm thinking that the closest this poor child will get to "A Lexus" is on the working side of a drive-thru window.

MARQUIS *(Pro: Mar-keez or Mar-kwees)*

Historically this is a name given to noblemen in various European countries. In America, it's the name of a Mercury automobile model built by Ford. This boy's name will conjure up thoughts of nobility, class and an overall vehicle rating of 6.5 out of 10 in US News & World Report.

JACEDES *(Pro: ja-say-dees)*

This girl's name combines the popular Spanish name element "JA" with Mercedes, a German manufacturer of luxury motor vehicles known for its technological and safety innovations. For her entire life this girl will have to repeat, and maybe spell, her name for everyone she meets. Thanks mom and dad.

TAVALON *(Pro: ta-va-lon)*

Avalon is the place where King Arthur's sword, Excalibur (this is another "good" name option), was made. It is also a popular vehicle made by Toyota. I'm told that "TA" is baby talk for "thank you". I suppose this child should be thankful that his mother didn't name him "TAPINTO"!

KIAWANA *(Pro: key-uh-wa-nuh)*

Kia is a Korean made automobile that apparently is a popular rental car in Tijuana. Odds are, that's also where little Kiawana was conceived.

AVANTI   *(Pro: uh-van-tee)*

Only 4,600 of these fiberglass body corvette engine automobiles were made. There probably was only one girl made with this name. Thank goodness!

KARHONDA   *(Pro: car-hon-duh)*

Honda makes affordable, quality cars, motorcycles and lawnmowers. I wonder which product line this child was name after?

Related name: Kryhonda

3

CLEVER MATCHES
CLEVER MATCHES (General)

Without any apparent regard for the emotional well being of their children, these parents thought it would be funny to match their child's first name with their family's last name to form a "clever" expression or statement. They were right! These kids' names are hysterical!

TOP NAMES

ASA SPADES
This child has only two possible career options - a Black Jack Dealer or a Wise Guy.

LEROY RUNS
I sure hope this kid can run track. Otherwise, I'm envisioning a recurring role on Cops.

POETRY BOOK
Coffee houses and jazz clubs are in this child's future, along with merciless teasing.

LAKE SALMONS
Another set of parents that should not have been allowed to spawn.

MIGHTY FINE
OMG! She had better be!!

SANDY HANDS
Ouch!

FUTURE BLANKS
A premonition of this child's future.

LULU MALLARD
I think her dad's name is Donald.

CANDY KANE
Sweet name!

MICHELIN FIRESTONE
Her parents must have been really been into rubber products… well, except in one instance!

CEDAR PULLEY
Wouldn't Steel have been a more appropriate first name?

CRYSTAL BALL
I see a blank future for this girl. Oh, sorry. I meant Future Blank.

YOUNG BOOZER
Don't you hate it when your parents think they are being funny but they really aren't.

ALEXANDER GREAT
Alexander is a great name! Alexander Great is _____ name? (This is the interactive portion of the book – suggestions: clever, ridiculous, asinine, etc.)

CLEVER MATCHES (Adult)

These names are particularly interesting because they are both clever and rude. I am fairly certain that if any of you share the same surname as these families, and decide to be as "clever", that your child will be spending more time on a therapist's couch than on the monkey bars at recess.

TOP NAMES

LES HEAD
Grooming their son to be the perfect husband one day, because his expectations for a certain adult activity will not be too demanding.

EASY MORE
Mom, I strongly suggest a pre-puberty visit to the OBGYN.

KISSAMEE CHERRY
Not an invitation that one regularly receives, but I'm guessing it's likely to be accepted more often than not.

LONG WANG
Obviously Dad played a major role in this naming process.

LITTLETON ORGAN
Sorry, Dude.

PETER DICK
Excuse me, but shouldn't there be a limit on the number of penis references in one person's name?

DICK NATURALE
It's good to know that this child is named for a "naturale" male body part.

DICK POUNDER
Please, is nothing sacred anymore!

DICK HOLDER

Whether male or female being called a dick holder cannot be a good thing.

KALEIGH KAME

Great, thanks for sharing!

4

SO, YOU WANT YOUR CHILD'S NAME TO BE REALLY DIFFERENT?

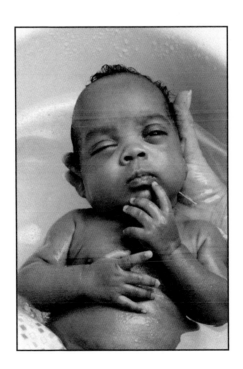

It takes a lot of nerve to give your child a name that is totally different from the norm. In doing so you could be subjecting your child to a lot of teasing from other children, and perhaps from some adults as well. However, a really "different" name can also be a source of pride for your child. It may also serve to bolster their sense of individuality. Further, if one day your child becomes famous, it's likely that he or she will be identifiable to the world by their first name alone! For example, Shaquille (Shaq), Beyonce, Shakira, Madonna, and **NEQUARIUS** (ok, she's not famous yet but...).

Having a really different name could pay off big one day. However, as with most things, where there is potential reward, there is also risk. The parents of the children in this chapter have rolled the dice with their kids' names. Here's a bit of free advice; if you're ever in Las Vegas with any one of these parents, bet opposite of whatever number they're wagering on.

TOP "REALLY DIFFERENT" NAMES

CHAVIOLEYETTE   *(Pro: shav-ee-oh-lee-et)*

What do you get when you combine a Chevy with a moist towelette?

GIGANTE   *(Pro: ji-gan-tee)*

Don't worry ... it's a boy. Whew!

LIMEJEL   *(Pro: lime-jel)*

Could she possibly be related to Limejello, Lemonjello and Orangello? Obviously not - she's missing an "o".

SHATARIUS   *(Pro: sha-tar-ee-us)*

Is this the astrological sign after Scorpio, or the one before Leo?

ROITAN   *(Pro: roy-tan)*

The very first name I ever collected. This one's for you, Pop!

LADORABLE

Beautiful name for a girl. Too bad he's a 6′ 5″ point guard.

UNIQUECA   *(Pro: u-nee-kwee-kwa)*

Only because someone thought the name Unique wasn't unique enough, do we have this masterpiece.

TRENDY   *(Pro: tren-dee)*

I really hope this name doesn't start a new trend of kids named Trendy.

DELECTA   *(Pro: dee-lec-tuh)*

DORCAS   *(Pro: door-cus)*

These people are just flat out cruel!

GLADLICIA   *(Pro: glad-li-shuh)*

I think I speak for all of us when I say that there are not enough names that end with "lisha."

ANDELICIA   *(Pro: an-duh-li-shuh)*

ECEDRIC   *(Pro: eh-ced-ric)*

This name gives me a headache.

DELONDER   *(Pro: duh-lon-der)*

Don't ponder over this name too long, you could become nauseas.

ARQUATTLAKIA   *(Pro: ar-kwat-lake-ee-uh)*

Oh the humanity!

CRAPHONSO   *(Pro: cra-fon-zo)*

Guess what his nickname will be? I'll give you a hint, it's the first 4 letters of his name.

TEBUCKY   *(Pro: tuh- buck-ee)*

How insensitive! Not everyone can afford braces.

CHIQUANIKA   *(Pro: che- kwa'-nee-kuh)*

DELISHA *(Pro: duh-lee-shuh)*

Yum!

STARSHEMA *(Pro: star-she-muh)*

THYISHACHOLENE *(Pro: thy-ee-shuh-sho-leen)*

This is your brain. THIS is your brain on drugs.

SHAQUANTA *(Pro: shuh-qwan-tuh)*

Hi, how are ya … Hi, how are ya …. Hi, how are ya ….

SUNDAY *(Pro: Sun-day)*

No one likes Monday, but everyone likes Sunday … well, except for a child named Sunday.

You may have noticed that some of these gems went without comment. All I can tell you is that even your author's vivid imagination has its limits.

5

HEE HAW

Where do we begin with this gaggle of names? Most likely in the hills of some states that are otherwise pretty nice places to live. Somehow, something got lost in the translation when these children were named. These are funny names created by people who either know they're being funny or, God forbid, just don't have a clue. As for me, I like most of these names. In fact, if I were choosing YOUR child's name I would strongly consider using one of the names in this chapter. Unfortunately, when our children were born there was not a sophisticated name resource like this publication to assist us in the naming process.

TOP NAMES

WALTERREAN *(Pro: wal-ter-een)*

I bet you thought all those stories about in-breeding were just rumors.

BREDFORD *(Pro: bred-ferd)*

There will never be any doubt where this child was bred. Wouldn't this make a great Ford commercial?

FAIRLEANA *(Pro: fare-lee-ann-uh)*

Fairleana, it's ok if you harbor some resentment towards your parents. In fact, I think that would be quite *Fair* under the circumstances.

EARSEL *(Pro: er-suhl)*

Well, I reckon that ol' Earl had a baby girl.

ERLEAN *(Pro: er-leen)*

Earl, you sure are good at making baby girls.

LORDELL *(Pro: lor-dell)*

I don't remember any story about the Lord meeting up with the Farmer in the Dell.

LAWANDER

(Pro: la-wan-der)

You may "wander" how they came up with this name. Well, first you take a normal, everyday word (wander) and then add a "La" to it. It's a very simple process. It must be because Lawander's parents figured it out.

HARKLES

(Pro: har-cull-s)

Hark the herald angels sing.

COY

(Pro: koi)

Cute name. Stupid, but cute.

OINT

(Pro: oint)

Suuuuuuuuuuueeeeeeeeey!

EARLVIN

(Pro: erl-vin)

A never-ending homage to Earl. Who can blame them?

VILLARD

(Pro: vill-erd)

"Earl, I think Willard is spelled with **a W"**.

LUVENNIA

(Pro: loo-vin-eee-uh)

LUEANN

(Pro: loo-ann)

LUEANDRA

(Pro: loo-ann-druh)

Say it with me, Louuuuuuuuuuuuuuuuuuuu!

GLEB

(Pro: gleb)

You think they meant to name him Glib? How about Glebe? Please help me here! What the heck is a Gleb? Is it curable?

VERLENE

(Pro: ver-leen)

Verlene, Verlene, ... don't take your love to town. Just get out of town.

LOSINA

(Pro: low-seen-uh)

Losina, run for the hills! Your parents have taken leave of their senses!

WILANDRA

(Pro: wil-ann-druh)

Will poor little Wilandra's parents ever realize what they've done here? Don't bet on it.

ENVER

(Pro: en-ver)

Goodness gracious! These people must've fallen off the tater wagon one too many times.

6

HOUSEHOLD ITEMS

The best thing about naming your child after a common household item is the plethora of choices you have right at your finger tips. Don't believe me? Just open your refrigerator and start naming what you see. Better yet, go to your bathroom and look around. That's what **TOILETTA'S** (actual name) mother must have done. No need to thank me. It's my pleasure to be of assistance to you.

Ladies and gentleman, without further ado, I present to you what has been chosen by those close to the author as one of the best chapters in our book. I wholeheartedly agree.

TOP NAMES

FAMIKA DINETTE (First and last name)   *(Pro: fa-mike-uh)*

The 1950's gave us a number of memorable things. Rock-n-roll, Hula Hoop and the Pill. It also gave us Formica Dinettes. The combination of these two household items proved to be a match made in heaven. Mom is obviously stuck in the 50s. Famika is likely to prefer granite.

LAVORIS   *(Pro: luh-vor-us)*

Somebody should get Lavoris's parents a big bottle and make them drink it.

LEMONJELLO   *(Pro: la-mon-je-lo)*

What would Bill Cosby say?
Similar names: **ORANGELLO** and **LIMEJELLO** (Can this get worse?)

DE'JEAN   *(Pro: dee-zhawn a.k.a. dijon)*

If you name your boy this, don't be surprised if he turns out to be a real wiener.

LATRINA   *(Pro: la-tree-nuh)*

Def: Spanish lavatory
I'm hoping that people don't crap all over this kid.

SHANDA LEER (First and last names)   *(Pro: shan-duh leer)*

Crystal, of course!

STERLING SILVA (First and last names)   *(Pro: stur-ling   sil-vuh)*

These parents must think of themselves as being very sophisticated people. What are the odds that little Sterling will end up tarnishing the family name?

SHAMONIA
(Pro: shuh-mohn-yuh)

This name really stinks!

CHIFFONETTA   *(Pro: Shi-fu-net-tuh)*

Apparently mom had her daughter's future prom on her mind when they asked her what her baby's name was. The nurse should have immediately called Planned Parenthood. Might as well get the process started early.

APPLE   *(Pro: a-pull)*

Good fruit; rotten name.

7

KEEP IT FORMAL

With business casual, dress-down Fridays, and all of the informal means of communicating these days, it's refreshing to see that some parents are trying to bring back some much needed civility and formality to our society.

If you want your child to spend his weekends at the yacht club or in the Hamptons, you will want to consider a name that will engender thoughts of "upper class" and "high society". Formal names like Quincy,

Brook and Ward scream sophistication. You may find that the "formal" names given to the children in this chapter scream something else. We'll let you fill in the missing word.

TOP NAMES

MISTER

(Pro: miss-ter)

What a stroke of genius on the part of Mister's parents. Think about it. No one could ever refer to Mister without calling him Mister. Whether you call him Mr. Mister Smith or Mister Smith, it's impossible to refer to him without saying his full name. It's a brain teaser!!! Throughout his life he will be Mr. Formal, or shall I say, Mister Formal.

SIR-ANTHONY

(Pro: sir-an-thon-eee)

Sir-Anthony may be even more formal than Mister. It wouldn't feel right speaking to this child without a simultaneous genuflect. "Thank you, Sir-Anthony", "Sir-Anthony, will you join me this weekend at the club?" Or, "May I get you a double martini, Sir-Anthony?" Some bowing needs to be going on when addressing this young man! This name oozes class. Even his nick-name, "Sir" portends upper crust. A thought ... What if he were to be knighted one day? He would be known as Sir Sir-Anthony (fill in the last name). You can't get more formal than that.

Similar names: Sir John, Sir Raphael, and Sir Louis (the new Three Musketeers)

SARGEANT   *(Pro: sar-jent)*

Most men have to enlist in the military and work hard to earn the rank of Sergeant. This young man has been given his rank right out of the womb. If he joins the military, I fear that his name may be an impediment to a military career. Private Sargeant or Captain Sargeant just doesn't sound right. However, Sargeant Sargeant would be beyond words. Awesome!

RATH   *(Pro: Rath)*

Oh rath, you're such a cad! There's just something wrong about naming a child Rath. One could see if his name was Rathbone. That's a classy old aristocratic name (I guess). But Rath? I have a funny feeling that his parents are going to experience the Wrath of Rath someday.

MAN   *(Pro: man)*

It's true. There is a male named "Man" and it's not short for Manuel or Manny. What can we say about a boy named Man? This isn't a "traditional" formal name like the others. However, being known as "The Man" can get you into some elite circles. Of course, you'll have to learn not to take it personal when you hear people railing against "The Man".

HONOR   *(Pro: on-er)*

Can't you just picture this courtroom scene: A young man standing before the bench and the judge saying, "You're Honor?" And the young man replies "Your Honor?" "Young man, you're Honor!?" "Like I said, your Honor". This could actually happen. Scout's Honor. Horrifying!

DEHONOR   *(Pro: de-on-er)*

Well, Dehonor is obviously when you've lost your honor, e.g, when the judge throws your rear end in jail for mocking him. However, if I had a vote, I think I'd rather lose my Honor than be named Dehonor.

8

A NEW TWIST

Taking a traditional name and adding a new wrinkle has become quite popular. If you stop for a second to think about it, it's really a great idea. Perhaps you would like to name your child after you or the child's other parent but don't want them to be known as Little Johnny or Betty, Jr., their entire lives. After all, everyone deserves their own identity. So, for example, if your name is Diane all you need do is add "netta" and you have **DIANETTA** (actual name) or add 'ia' and you have **DIANIA** (actual name). Of course, some parents have taken this whole "add a twist" thing too far. I know you are shocked by this. However, there is no way you can anticipate how shocked you will be after seeing the results of some parents' twisted thought process.

TOP NAMES

MARSHAMELLE *(Pro: mar-shuh-mel)*

Either dad's name is Mel or these folks are really into campfires.

RODGERILL *(Pro: ra-jur-ill)*

Don't worry. I checked up on Roger last week and he's feeling much better.

SHYANNA *(Pro: Shi-an-uh)*

These parents must have felt that if they included the word "shy" in their daughter's name that it would result in her being an extrovert. You know, reverse psychology. Now, that's real genius, folks. Following their logic, I'd suggest that if you want your kid to go to a top notch university one day that you add 'dumb' or 'stupid' to your child's name, e.g, Dumbdavid or Stupidsara. I can hear the Directors of Admissions calling now!

PHILNESHA *(Pro: fill-ne-shuh)*

Phil = Good name.   Philnesha = bad name.

QWANDRA *(Pro: kwan-druh)*

The recipe for this name is simple: 1 = Wanda   +   1 = Q   +   1 = R When done, enjoy the uniqueness of your daughter's name. Bon appétit!

BENJAMESE

(Pro: ben-ja-meece)

Japanese, Burmese, Chinese, Siamese, Benjamese.

JAEMES

(Pro: james)

I'm going to go out on a limb here and say that neither one of these parents ever won a spelling bee.

KIMITHA

(Pro: kim-eee-thuh)

Nice work Kim. Your daughter's name will be unique amongst her friends until they start calling her Kim. Oops!

KEITHA

(Pro: keeth-uh)

Dad must have loved his name so much that he couldn't bare the thought of his little girl not sharing it with him. Could Timitha and Tomitha be far behind?

VIOLETTA

(Pro: vi-oh-let-uh)

Who else besides me thinks that Violetta has been violated by her parents?

CHASSIDY

(Pro: cha-si-dee)

For you car nuts out there.

DARRAIL

(Pro: duh-rail)

Darrail, you've been railroaded!

RONRICO *(Pro: ron-rico)*

Ron and Rico go together like Rum and Coke.

DA'BRIANNA *(Pro: da-bree-on-uh)*

This name is so versatile that it would fit into three chapters of this book: Apostrophes, Daddy's Little Girl, and A New Wrinkle. Thank you Da'Mom and Da'Dad for your stellar contribution!

CHARLESZEETA *(Pro: char-elz-zet-uh)*

Hey Chuck! I know you were hoping for a boy, but …..

DONTRA *(Pro: don-truh)*

"Tra" is a combination of letters traditionally used at the beginning of a name. Travis and Trajon are two fine examples of this. Using TRA at the end of your child's name is not as popular. I can't imagine why.

APRELL *(Pro: a-prell)*

Remember Prell? If you answered yes you must be over 40.

CLOTHILDA *(Pro: claw-thil-duh)*

Come on. Isn't Hilda bad enough? Even people named Hilda hate their name.

TODRIKA *(Pro: tod-ree-kuh)*

Tod, I'd be interested in your thought process on this one.

9

LA LA LA LA LA LA LA LA LA MEANS I LOVE YOU

What a great old song by The Delfonics. As you will soon find out, if you put "La" in front of any other letters in the alphabet, no matter what order the letters are in, it creates a truly lovely name. Best of all, the list of potential names is limitless! Seriously, I would not lie to you. Believe me when I tell you that the things I am saying are true, and the way I explain them to you, yes to you, listen to me, La La La La La La La La La means I love you.

TOP "LA" NAMES

LaFREESHA   *(Pro: la-free-shuh)*

Def: Loves cold weather.

LaKEIZER   *(Pro: la-key-zur)*

Def: Loves cranky old men.

LaMIA   *(Pro: lay-me-uh)*

Def: Loves sex.
Query, is it prudent to have your daughter's name contain the words "lay me"?

LaMONTE   *(Pro: la-mon-tay)*

Def: Lamont Sanford's sister on Sanford and Son
Don't say anything, but I think Grady was her biological father.

LaPASSION *(Pro: la-pa-shun)*

Def: Loves passion
Mom and Dad may want to look in to whether they are still making chastity belts. Just a suggestion.

LaPETHA *(Pro: la-pee-thuh)*

Def: Loves all things associated with urine.
Would someone please call children's services!

LaPONDA *(Pro: la-pon-duh)*

Def: Loves all bodies of water, but particularly ponds.
Reminds me of the movie, On Golden Ponda.

LaRONALD *(Pro: la-ron-uld)*

Def: Loves all men named Ronald.
Don't laugh. One day this girl may end up marrying a fast food chain icon with bushy red hair and big yellow clown shoes.

LaRUINTA *(Pro: la-runt-uh)*

Def: The runt of the litter.
Did this really need to be said?

LaSHAWANDA *(Pro: la-sha-wan-duh)*

Def: Loves the letter "A".
I can hear mom saying, "Let's see how many A's we can squeeze in to one name!"

LaSONEE   (Pro: la-so-nay)

Def: Loves sonar equipment.
This will come in handy when she's trying to get away from the dummies who named her.

LaTARSHA   (Pro: la-tar-shuh)

Def: Loves the smell of tar.
Who doesn't? This could explain the name selection.

LaTRAIL   (Pro: la-trayl)

Def: Loves hiking trails.
Also would be a great name for a heart healthy Hispanic snack food, "LaTrail Mix".

LaVASIA   (Pro: la-vey-zhuh)

Def: Loves all things Vasian. Sorry, I meant to say Asian.

LaJUANNA   (Pro: la-jon-uh)

Def: Loves the john.
How special! What's with the veiled slang expression for a toilet? At least TOILETTA'S parents had the decency to come right out with it.

~~~~~~~~~~

Other Notable "La" Names

LaVontrae	*(Pro: la-von-tray)*	**LaTesha**	*(Pro: la-te-shuh)*
Lamoni	*(Pro: la-mon-ay)*	**LaVondrae**	*(Pro: la-von-dray)*
Laphina	*(Pro: la-fee-nuh)*	**Lawanna**	*(Pro: la-wan-uh)*
LaQuinnia	*(Pro: la-qwin-ee-uh)*	**LaMichael**	*(Pro: la-my-cull)*
Lashone	*(Pro: la-show-nay)*	**LaBarbara**	*(Pro: la-bar-bra)*

— **10** —

MEDICAL

This will be our shortest chapter. There is good reason for that. Despite what you have otherwise read in this book, I would like to think that the majority of parents are reasonable people who would not want to name their child after a disease or body part. Of course, I've been wrong before. These children's mothers must have still been under the effects of their epidurals when they came up with these names. I shudder to think that there is any other plausible explanation.

TOP NAMES

MECONIUM   *(Pro: mi-koh-nee-uhm)*

Def: Newborn baby fecal matter.
There will come a day when this little girl from Ohio finds out that she was named after the bile, mucous, and goo that she ingested in her mother's womb and then expelled through her rear end after she was born. I bet that when she confronts mom, mom will for the first time know the meaning of that intriguing and exotic sounding word that she heard the nurse's discussing in the hallway. Won't she feel like crap!

PLACENTA   *(Pro: pluh-sen-tuh)*

Def: Afterbirth
And you thought Meconium was disgusting! Yes, nothing says, "I love you" more than naming your baby girl after an organ that was involved in your baby's waste elimination and then spontaneously expelled itself after you gave birth. This name rolls right off of your tongue, doesn't it? Maybe mom meant to name her **POLENTA** (actual name). Give her a break; anyone could make that mistake.

MALERIA   *(Pro: muh-lair-ee-uh)*

Def: Malaria is a disease spread by mosquitoes that has claimed the lives of millions of people.
One could only hope that naming their daughter Maleria doesn't come back to bite them in the rear end one day.

— 11 —

MULTIPLES

What a blessing it is to give birth to multiple children at the same time. It's also a blessing to be able to select more than one name from all of the beautiful boy's and girl's names that are available, like **PHENNORIS**, and **LIQUIDA** (actual names). All kidding aside (sure), it is a great opportunity to choose 2 or more names that you really like and would have had a hard time choosing between if you just had one baby.

As you will see, these parents took a different approach to naming their multiples, with interesting results. Although these parents were blessed with this opportunity, their children may end up feeling more cursed than blessed.

TOP MULTIPLES NAMES

WONDERFUL and MARVELOUS

I'm quite certain that these little girls reflect their names. My concern is that using adjectives like these for your child's name can be quite risky. In this instance, anything less than astonishing and exciting, positive conduct, will be a big disappointment. Imagine the snide comments from friends, teachers and employers (if anyone will hire them with these names). I'm guessing mom's name was "Blissfully Ignorant".

REYONTE and RAYONTE   (Pro: ree-on-tay   and   ray-on-tay)

Apparently "onte" is a slanderous playground term that is used at times as an alternative for a certain four letter word. Here's hoping that these parents didn't know this fact before sticking "onte" onto Rey and Ray. I'm betting that some of their playmates will have it figured out by the time they reach age 10. Ouch!

BRITTNEY and BRITANICA

These folks are obviously Britophiles. The real issue is why they would want to give their twins names that have the same nickname. Isn't looking alike and having the same birthday enough to deal with already?

VERY, TRULY and REALLY

I'll give you one guess at the last name of these unfortunate triplets. No, it's not "Stupid". That's what their parents were. Ok, here you go, it's SWEET! Yes, Very Sweet, Truly Sweet and Really Sweet. Stop laughing! The only thing that one can say about these names is that they are very, truly and really ridiculous. Too bad stoning is no longer permitted. I think Mother Sweet would be in trouble!

SPECIAL

Mom must have chosen this name just in case anyone ever questioned whether her little girl was "Special." OMG!

12

HYPHENATED NAMES

Hyphenated surnames are common these days. The prevailing thought is that married people want to maintain their individual identity, yet still show their commitment to the person they love. However, hyphenated first names are a whole different ballgame. For reasons unknown to most of us, adding a hyphen, i.e., dash, to one's child's first name, is becoming a popular cultural phenomenon. Thankfully for all of you, I have figured out why the dash (-) is finding it's way into the middle of our kids' names. How could I express this for you in both an informative, yet tasteful manner? The nicest thing I can say is to quote a very famous political figure who once said, "It must be silly season!" Now silly isn't the first word that came to mind upon collecting these names. However, if you think about it, hyphenating your child's name gives you the opportunity to give your child two first names, plus a middle name! This way, if you are stuck on a few names that you really like, you can just add a dash between them and voila', a new name is born with all of your favorite names combined! Let's try a few out: Tom-Dick (Harry), Huey-Duey (Louie), and Moe-Larry (Curly). These are obviously all great new name possibilities. However, perhaps you will want to consider some of the more "traditional" hyphenated names below.

TOP HYPHENATED NAMES

LA - SHA   *(Pro: la-dash-uh)*

No, you haven't misread the pronunciation. This girl's name includes a four letter word that isn't spelled out in her name. It's actually quite clever if you think about it. Here's a hyphenated word that this girl may have for her parents that also includes an unwritten four letter word: F –You!

J-AVON and J-TRICE   *(Pro: juh-von and juh-treece)*

I personally prefer Mary Kay.

SEDONNA-REE   *(Pro: suh-done-uh-ree)*

At first glance I thought these people named their daughter after Sedona, one of America's most beautiful cities. Upon closer observation it became apparent that these people simply didn't know what in the hell they were doing.

JON-LEESA   *(Pro: jon-lee-suh)*

Another gender confused child in the making.

I-NJERI   *(Pro: in-jer-ee)*

Me, Tarzan. You, Jane. I, Njeri!

DEX-ANN   *(Pro: dex-ann)*

What an abomination. Someone should have to answer for this.

MASHEHA-KEYE   *(Pro: muh-shee-ha-kee)*

Did these people honestly think this was a good name combination?

TUY-SHAWN   *(Pro: tie-shawn)*

Another set of parents screwing up a perfectly good name.

E-BAY   *(Pro: eee-bay)*

I'll bet if you had thought about it for a minute that you could have guessed someone would name their child after the world's most popular online market place. I heard that in order to communicate with this kid, you first need to provide her with your name, address and telephone number. Thereafter, a password must be established between the two of you. Also, you will have to provide her with an existing credit card. Finally, ask yourself, can anyone really be so crazy as to name their child E-Bay? Unfortunately, the answer is yes.

DE-DONGIO   *(Pro: dee-dong-eee-o)*

Def: The Dong. Either Vietnamese currency or a nickname for male genitalia.

MAR-QUAN   *(Pro: mar-qwan)*

This name needed a hyphen. Marquan is just so 90's.

JON-METRIUS   *(Pro: jon-me-tree-us)*

Does this name remind you of a gladiator movie, or is it just me?

MAYANA-JAE   *(Pro: may-yon-uh-jay)*

May you never choose this name for your child.

K-SEAN   *(Pro: kay-shawn)*

Maybe this was a typographical error and there was supposed to be a period after the K. Or maybe, K-Sean's mom was an avid K-Mart shopper!

13

ROYALTY

Americans are fascinated with the world's royalty. You can hardly walk by a newsstand without seeing Lady Di's boys or some Princess on the cover of your favorite gossip magazine. Remember Fergie, Dutchess of whatever, and how popular she was? Throughout history, Royalty has been involved in some of the most notorious scandals. Like Prince Charles and Camilla's affair which spawned the, "I want to live in your bloomers" line. Please tell me he didn't really say that. Their bad behavior, adulterous affairs, and weird quirks are legendary. That's why it fascinates me that some people would want their children's name associated with anything royal. I can understand naming your German Sheppard **PRINCE** (actual name) or your cat **QUEENIE** (actual name), but your kids? Here's some good name options for you royalphiles. You know who you are.

TOP ROYALTY NAMES

JO'MAGESTY and JERMAGESTY

(Pro: jo-maj-est-ee and jer-maj-est-ee)

If you're not laughing, you need help. These young men have been put on equal footing with all of the world's royalty from the moment they were born. Just picture what a meeting between our boys and Queen Elizabeth would be like. It might go something like this:

Jo'Magesty:	Pleased to meet you, Your Majesty.
Jermagesty:	Your Majesty, it's an honor to meet you.
Queen Elizabeth:	Pleased to meet you, Jo'Magesty.
Queen Elizabeth:	The honor is all mine, Jermagesty.

These names are truly regal! What other names do you know that automatically come with loyal subjects?

CLEOPATRIA *(Pro: cle-o-pa-tree-uh)*

A take-off on Cleopatra, the Queen of Egypt. She was known for her shrewdness and ugly masculine features. Yet somehow she managed to seduce both Caesar and Marc Antony, two of ancient Rome's most powerful men. I guess Cleopatria would be a good name choice for your little girl if you're expecting her to come up a little short in the looks department. Who knows, she could rule the world one day! Let's just hope it's not by the same means as her namesake.

ROYAL DAPPER *(Pro: roy-ul da-per)*

This fellow would have been included in the Clever Match chapter, but for the sheer regalness of his name. He is both royal and dapper. He must feel so special.

ISIS *(Pro: ahy-sis)*

Isis was a goddess in ancient Egyptian religious beliefs and a sexy super hero in the 1970's TV series, "The Secrets of Isis." In the television series, she spent most of her time kicking the crap out of various bad people. If you choose this name for your daughter, I'd suggest that as soon as she starts walking that you enroll her in a self-defense class; she's probably going to need it.

PRINCETTA *(Pro: prin-set-uh)*

Ok, Dads, we all think of our little girls as princesses. However, who among you would have the _____ to name your daughter Princetta? Thought so.

TIERA   *(Pro: tee-ar-uh)*

It's never too early to start grooming your daughter for the beauty pageant circuit. After all, there's just so many positive experiences and qualities that a young girl can gain from being involved in beauty pageants, e.g, Bulimia, Anorexia, Stage Moms, Back Stabbing, Pedophilia, Bitchiness and Stupidity, just to name a few.

Spin-off Name: **LETEARA**   *(Pro: lay-tee-ar-uh)*

— 14 —

WE NEED MORE APOSTROPHES

There are many things that we need here in the Unites States. We need a cleaner environment. We need more jobs. We need lower gas prices. We need more funny baby names! Often overlooked amongst our needs is the need for more apostrophes. That's right; the full potential of the apostrophe is not being met. The tragic under-usage of the apostrophe has plagued America for years. Some may say we need more cowbell, but that's just not so. Cowbells are cool and romantic. But apostrophes add class and panache to every word they are associated with. They accent our lives. Speaking for myself (and those of you afraid to admit it), I can never get enough apostrophes!

As most of you know, an apostrophe is a punctuation mark traditionally used to indicate the omission of a letter from a word, a possessive, or a plural. In this chapter, we have names that contain apostrophes. The challenge is to figure out what the purpose of these seemingly randomly inserted apostrophes are. None of the apostrophes appear to fit any of the typical reasons why people use apostrophes.

Now, although I'm an advocate for both the increased and out-of-the-box use of apostrophes, I cannot and will not tolerate their misuse'. I'm hoping' that you'll be able to find some j'ustification for thes'e parents inser'tion of apostrophes' in their childrens names'. I'm having a' hard enough time just trying' to f'igure ou't what these names mean.

TOP APOSTROPHE NAMES

SHA'HADA   (Pro: sha ha-da)

Def: HADA - Help, Another Dumb Ass parent.

CHA'LLANE   (Pro: sha-lane)

Def: Sade mated with Jack LaLanne.

SHARE'E   (Pro: sha-ray)

Def: A game in which words are acted out and you have to guess the word.

E'TIENNE   *(Pro: a-'tee-en)*

French sounding name that none of her friends or teachers will ever be able to spell or pronounce.

D'ARCO   *(Pro: dee-arco)*

Def: An over-abundance of gas.
How special!

LE' MAR   *(Pro: la-mar)*

Def: A chronic inflammatory connective tissue disease that defaces the body.

CHERRE'E   *(Pro: shar-ree)*

Def: Lovely as a summer day, distant as the Milky Way.

SHA' QUEETHA   *(Pro: sha-kwee-tha)*

Def: Daughter of Queetha

SHAN'TON   *(Pro: shan-tawn)*

Def: Weighs a ton.
Hope this one's a boy!

DENE'T   *(Pro: danay-tee)*

Duh whattee?

TY' LEI   *(Pro: tie-lee)*

Hope her friends don't take her name literally!

RIY' YAD   *(Pro: ree-yad)*

Def: The capital of Saudi Arabia - sort of.

WA'MEKIA   *(Pro: wa-me-key-uh)*

I have no earthly idea what this name means!

T'KEYMA   *(Pro: tuh-key-muh)*

Another example of why sniffing glue is bad for you.

DA'JAVONNE   *(Pro: day-jay-von)*

I'm guessing that there will not be a Day that goes by that Da'Jayvonne isn't going to wonder why they did this to him.

15

DADDY'S LITTLE GIRL

Dad's just love their little girls. They are like miniature versions of the woman they fell in love with. Dads also have a special relationship with their sons. For fathers, sons are much easier to name than daughters because there is always a fallback selection available, i.e, dad's name. However, what if dad does not have the son he's always wanted and, therefore, no one to pass his name on to? This is where things can get interesting. There's a popular song titled "Daughters." One of the verses is, "Fathers be good to your daughters." When it came time to name their little girls, these fathers were not so good to their daughters.

TOP "DADDY'S LITTLE GIRL" NAMES

SHERRONDA   *(Pro: she-on-duh)*   Daughter of Sherrod

"Help, Sherronda. Help, help Sherronda. Help me get her out of my heart".

Rhonda? I think the Beach Boys made a big mistake!

SHERMAINE   *(Pro: sher-main)*   Daughter of Sherman

Sherman, WTF?

TAMERO   *(Pro: ta-mare-oh)*   Daughter of Tomero

Tomero, you should have let your name, and any derivative thereof, die with you.

NATE'   *(Pro: na-te')*   Daughter of Nate

Nate, I know that you were going for a French twist on your girl's name, but did you ever consider that most kids are going to call her Nate? I suppose this name does have a certain *je ne sais quoi* though!

MAXILIA   *(Pro: ma- ill-yuh)*   Daughter of Max

Max, does your daughter even speak to you?

CHYRELLA   *(Pro: chai-rell-uh)*   Daughter of Chyron

Hold on, I think I'm getting sick.

ROBERTHA *(Pro: ro-ber-thuh)* Daughter of Robert

This name lacks complete imagination, Robert! Worse than that, your daughter's nickname will likely be "Berta." Sexy!

LARMONSHELL *(Pro: lar-mon-shell)* All Daughters
LARMONDRIEL *(Pro: lar-mon-dree-el)* of Larmondo
LARMERJA *(Pro: lar-mer-juh)*

Larmondo, your name sucks and you have a cruel sense of humor. I'd sleep with the lights on if I were you.

JOELINDA *(Pro: jo-lin-duh)* Daughter of Joe

Dad was kind enough to share the naming rights to his daughter's name with his wife. I think I just found that couple who start pumping their fists when Harper Valley PTA comes on the radio.

RODNEISHA *(Pro: rod-nee-shuh)* Daughter of Rodney

Nice job, Rodney! …..the author says sarcastically.

ROBNEISHA *(Pro: rob-nee-shuh)* Daughter of Rob

What's with the "neisha" love fest? Maybe these guys should have just adopted some boys.

JEFFONIA *(Pro: jeff-o-nee-uh)* Daughter of Jeffery

If I didn't know better, I would have thought this was the name of some small town in Kentucky. Unfortunately, it's the name of some little girl called Jeff.

DONLETTE *(Pro: don-let)* Daughter of Donald

Don, if you have any compassion at all, please "Let" your daughter change her name

SCOTTRA *(Pro: sca-truh)* Daughter of Scott

Scott, this is really a dumb name. Seriously, I'm not kidding.

— 16 —

UNBELIEVABLE BUT TRUE, NAMES THAT BEGIN WITH "Q" AND "U"

People whose names begin with Q or U are very rare. That's because there just are not that many names in the US that begin with those letters. Quinn and Ursula are two of the best known and most traditional of Q and U names. Do not fret, however. For those of you enamored with the idea of using one of these letters to begin your child's name, some Unharnessed parents have blazed a trail for you. Let me warn you though - should you take the Quantum leap of choosing a Questionable name that begins with either of these letters, you may be asked to Quantify the basis for your Unfortunate decision so that will not they Quarantine you in a mental health facility for your Undiscerning judgment.

TOP "Q" NAMES

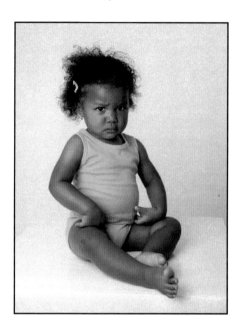

QUANTINA *(Pro: kwan-tee-nuh)*

Some say QUAN means "love, community, money and respect". **QUANTINA** means that your parents aren't the sharpest knives in the drawer.

QUANTRILLA *(Pro: kwan-tril-uh)*

There appears to be a movement to make up names incorporating the term "quan". The name Quantrilla is a darn good reason to stop the movement.

QUANZELLA *(Pro: kwan-zel-uh)*

Is there anyone besides me experiencing a mental picture of Godzilla right now?

QUA QUA   *(Pro: kwa-kwa)*

Qua Qua, you need to have a long discussion with your parents. Better yet, maybe you should just skip the discussion and have them probated.

QUE-QUE   *(Pro: kwee- kwee)*

Que Que, don't even think about asking your parents how they came up with this name. Just run! Run, Que-Que, run!

QUEAQUA   *(Pro: kwee-kwa)*

Honestly, her name isn't even pronounced like it's spelled! This just ain't right!

QUASHAWN   *(Pro: kway-shawn)*

Really? Why?

QUINTESSENCE   *(Pro: kwin-tess-ince)*

Def: The most essential part of something.
This name is the quintessence of parental idiocy.

QUINTOSA   *(Pro: kwin-to-suh)*

Combining Quinn (typically Irish name) with a pint of mimosa. Ok, so it's not Guiness, but at this point in the book I could use one.

QUAVADIS *(Pro: kway-vay-dis)*

Your guess is as good as mine.

TOP "U" NAMES

ULICIOUS *(Pro: yoo-lish-us)*

Much more than delicious, she's **ULICIOUS**!

UNEEDA *(Pro: yoo-nee-duh)*

Uneeda, sorry to tell you this, but you need-a new name!

UNIQUE *(Pro: yoo-neek)*

Just by being named Unique, this child will be just that. Naming your child with an appropriate positive adjective beginning with the letter U is not as easy as it looks. Let me give it a try: Unruly, Unhappy, Unessential. See what I mean?

UVONKIA *(Pro: yoo-von-kee-uh)*

If her parents were Russian, I could understand the name. But they're from Indiana!

UKEISHA *(Pro: yoo-kee-shuh)*

Keisha is a very popular name. Ukeisha? I'm guessing not so much.

UYNITILLA *(Pro: yoo-ni-till-uh)*

Parents, "you" deserve a thrashing if you name your daughter Uynitilla.

— 17 —

SIBLINGS

Having the opportunity to name more than one child is both a privilege and a potential mine field. After all, if you were to name one of your children a beautiful name like Olivia, naming her sister **ROTUNDA** might be the source of some tension between the siblings. To avoid these potential pitfalls, some parents develop themes for naming their offspring, like naming all of their children using the same first letter, for example, Megan, Mark and Matthew. Unfortunately, some parents have taken the "theme" idea and abused it to fit their own personal mantras or proclivities. As with many of the parents in this book, these parents should have been required to get a license before being allowed to procreate.

TOP "SIBLING" NAMES

DREADLESS and **DREADNAUGHT**   *(Pro: dred-les   and   dred-nawt)*

"Fear-less" and "Fear-not"
In speaking with Mom, she said that the inspiration for her sons' names was her desire that they would not be fearful of anything. I would say that there is no reason to fear using these names for your children so long as you have a great health insurance policy.

JUVIS and **JUDAS**   *(Pro: ju-vis   and jud-dus)*

Def: A symbol for a Juniper tree in Virginia and the disciple that betrayed Jesus.
It takes a real genius to pair these names up as, on the surface, they appear to have no connection.   However, Judas betrayed Jesus in the Garden of Gethsemane. Juniper trees are traditional trees used in middle east gardens. The Garden of Gethsemane was located in the Middle East. Now do you see the connection? Don't you wish you were this bright? By the way, it might not be a great idea to name your child after one of the bad guys in the Bible.

DEONTE' and **DEVONTE'**   *(Pro: dee-on-tay   and   de-von-tay)*

There is a theme here if you look closely. Let me save you the time. Both of these boys' names start with "De", end with "onte", and have an accent mark at the end for no apparent reason. Pretty obvious now that you know.

DAQUIRI, BRANDY, TEQUILA and CHAMPAGNE

So, mom and dad like to party a little bit. What's the problem? It could have been worse. They could have named their daughters: Orgasm, Leg Spreader, Sex on the Beach, and Slow Comfortable Screw. See what I mean?

GOD and EMPRESS

An empress is the female ruler of an empire and was often thought of as a god. God is well, God.   In an effort to give a huge vitamin B injection to the self-esteem of their little boy and girl, these nut jobs have managed to offend the creator of the universe and supreme being. Good luck, God, living up to that name! I bet you wish you had the power to smite your parents. Empress, all I can say is mazel tov.

SPECIAL, SPARKLE and STAR

Can't you see it now, sequined tutus, pink ballet shoes, and brightly colored batons strewn all about the house?   All three names are unique and we are at least aware of one well known person with the name "Star."   Maybe it's just me, but wouldn't you just love to give mom a "What were you thinking?" slap to the back of her head?

18

RELIGIOUS

Naming your child after a religious belief or common religious term can be seen as a sign of your faith. Perhaps your hope is that, as your child grows up, he or she will adopt the same belief system that you have. If you bestow upon your child any the names that are in this chapter, it may be a stretch to think that your kid will follow in your devotional pursuits. Rather, after your child figures out the cruel joke you played on them, you may want to think about moving away and "forgetting" to give them your new address. Don't say I didn't warn you.

TOP RELIGIOUS NAMES

PSIN   (Pro: sin)

Def: A departure from a divine command
In certain faiths you have what are called venial sins and mortal sins. Venial sins are lesser pardonable sins. Mortal sins are very serious sins such as unjustifiably taking another person's life. I'm not quite sure what kind of sin Psin's parents committed when they named him Psin. Let's hope he doesn't commit a mortal sin against his parents. Perhaps their saving grace will be their son's cool nickname - Pissin. Yikes!

HEAVEN   (Pro: hev-uhn)

"Heaven I'm in Heaven, and my heart beats so that I can hardly speak ...."

Def: An Irving Berlin song and what Heaven's boyfriend said to her when they finally hooked up.

GENESIS   (Pro: jen-uh-sis)

Def: A popular rock band featuring Phil Collins and Peter Gabriel. Not sure what this name has to do with religion, but someone told me it belonged in this chapter.

A MIRACLE *(Pro: a-meer-uh-kull)*

It will be a miracle if this child survives 5th grade recess.

OCEAN-MIRACLE *(Pro: oh-shuhn-mir-uh-kull)*

Another beautiful hyphenated name; most likely the child of some hippie leftovers from the 60s.

GOD *(Pro: God)*

He's still Empresses' brother from the Siblings chapter, and I'm still betting that his parents are in for a real smiting.

DE'MON *(Pro: day'mon)*

A note to De'Mon's mom: Look, I know that you thought this name sounded cool when you foisted it upon your little boy. However, did you even consider the possibility that he will be called Demon? You know, the devil! There could be hell to pay for selecting this name.

19

BEST OF THE REST

This chapter contains over 100 names that are just as **UNIQUE** and "interesting" as the others, but for the most part do not fit into a particular category. Although maybe **SHELFUNDA** could be in the Household Items chapter? In any event, these names are in a category of their own known as, "The Best of the Rest!"

TOP NAMES

~ A ~

Aquaneeta (Pro: ak-wuh-net-uh)

Atilah (Pro: uh-til-uh)

… As in, "The Hun"

Arjameka (Pro: ar-ju-mee-kuh)

~ B ~

Brenita (Pro: bruh-nee-tuh)

Breyanda (Pro: bray-on-duh)

Burnetta (Pro: ber-net-uh)

What did Netta do to deserve this?

~ C ~

Calleous   (Pro: kal-uhs)

How calleous of his parents!

Cavicia   (Pro: ka-vi-she-uh)

Ceilnor   (Pro: seal-nor)

Charard   (Pro: sha-rard)

I think it's a vegetable - Swiss Charard?

Chencata   (Pro: shen-ca-tuh)

Sounds like a new Latin dance.

Christshanda   (Pro: krist-shan-duh)

Cyntoria   (Pro: sin-toe-ree-uh)

Crayshon   (Pro: kray-shawn)

~ D ~

Daborlek *(Pro: dab-or-leek)*

Danquayle *(Pro: dan-kweyl)*

Named after an extremely popular vice-president.

Darsheria *(Pro: dar-shair-ee-uh)*

Deaullandte *(Pro: dee-yoo-i-on-tay)*

Really?

Decubinese *(Pro: dee-coo-bi-neece)*

Either a dish served at an upscale restaurant or a bedsore.

Daajee *(Pro: day-jee)*

~ E ~

Ediwuan *(Pro: ed-i-wan)*

Elvonda *(Pro: el-von-duh)*

There should be more names that start with "El". Come on people, I'm counting on you!

Erskala *(Pro: erk-sal-uh)*

Erandon *(Pro: er-an-don)*

Just remove a B and add an E - another New Twist!

Enjonee *(Pro: en-jon-ee)*

~ F ~

Frazell *(Pro: fra-zell)*

Falashade' *(Pro: fa-la-shuh-day)*

Folando *(Pro: fo-lan-do)*

I'm sure you've seen this name before. No? Does Tony Folando and Dawn ring a bell?

Fraquan *(Pro: fra-kwan)*

Very classy.

Furquan *(Pro: fur-kwan)*

Just when you thought a name couldn't get any classier than Fraquan.

~ G ~

Gonzola *(Pro: gon-zo-luh)*

A commonly used combination of a Venetian boat and cheese.

Guipage *(Pro: gui-peyl)*

Guipago *(Pro: gui-pa-jo)*

~ H ~

Haniel *(Pro: han-ule)*

Seriously folks, why ruin a perfectly good name?

Hershelly *(Pro: her-shell-ee)*

Either this name is the female version of Hershel or a misspelling of Hershey. Either way, my advice is, "Don't go there!"

Harrius *(Pro: har-ee-us)*

What in the heck is a Harrius? Is it next to the Mannoris?

Hashond *(Pro: ha-shon-d)*

Hermesha *(Pro: her-mee-shuh)*

~ I ~

Iesha *(Pro: i-ee-shuh)*

Ikumba *(Pro: i-cum-buh)*

We've all heard of the Rumba, but who amongst you knows the Ikumba!

Isophine *(Pro: i-so-feen)*

~ J ~

A cornucopia of funny names! No, cornucopia is <u>not</u> a person's name. How could you even think such a thing?

JaJa *(Pro: ja-ja)*

Jacquettta   *(Pro: ja-kwe-tuh)*

Are you shi- - - -g me?

Jaleelah   *(Pro: ja-lee-luh)*

Jazzlyn   *(Pro: jaz-lin)*

Jerquez   *(Pro: jur-kwez)*

Jillisa   *(Pro: jil-ee-suh)*

Do you think they took the parenting test? Ok, do you think they passed the parenting test?

Jocasta   *(Pro: jo-ka-suh)*

A new card game.

Joruth   *(Pro: jo-rooth)*

Jqueaqua   *(Pro: ku-kwan-uh)*

I guess Queaqua was too bland.

Juniesha   *(Pro: ju-nee-shuh)*

~ K ~

Kaelilia   *(Pro: kay-lie-luh)*

Keeoma   *(Pro: kee-oh-muh)*

Keomi   *(Pro: kee-oh-mee)*

Keezy   *(Pro: key-zee)*

Knekesha   *(Pro: ne-keyshuh)*

The first K is silent, in case you were wondering.

~ L ~

Le Shaunte'   *(Pro: la-shawn-tay)*

Ligea   *(Pro: lie-gee-uh)*

Lie whata?

Linstero   *(Pro: lin-stur-o)*

Liquida   (Pro: li-kwee-duh)

Wonder what kind of "liquid" her parents were consuming when they came up with this one?

Luretha   (Pro: lur-ree-thuh)

R-E-S-P-E-C-T!

Lueanra   (Pro: loo-on-ruh)

Luayaudrill   (Pro: loo-ay-uh-dril)

How in the world did they come up with this name?

Litho   (Pro: li-tho)

Graph?

~ M ~

Macquell   (Pro: ma-kwel)

Maereathra   (Pro: may-ree-thruh)

This name could have been worse. No way, you say? How about MaeUrethra? Never challenge the author!

Malio *(Pro: muh-lee-oh)*

Mannoris *(Pro: muh-nor-is)*

What is a mannoris? It sounds disgusting!

Marvella *(Pro: mar-vel-uh)*

Montaz *(Pro: mon-taz)*

Give these people credit, it takes a lot of effort to fit a "Z" in to a name.

Monshaye *(Pro: mon-shay)*

Meosha *(Pro: mee-oh-shuh)*

~ N ~

Nautica *(Pro: nau-ti-kuh)*

Norlanda *(Pro: nor-lan-duh)*

~ O ~

These all sound like foreign names, but you'll be happy to know that they are all your fellow Americans!

Otoniel *(Pro: oh-ton-eel)*

Otuka *(Pro: oh-tuh-kuh)*

Olarike *(Pro: oh-la-reek)*

Exactly!

Olatunya *(Pro: oh-la-too-nuh)*

No young lady should have to deal with a name that could be construed as containing the word "tuna".

~ P ~

Pashen *(Pro: pa-shun)*

Peshawn *(Pro: pee-shawn)*

How would you like everyone always telling you to pee? That's a lot of pressure!

~ Q ~

All of the Q names were depleted for our Q chapter. Hey, I think I just stumbled upon a potential new name: Depleted!

~ R ~

Radshowd *(Pro: rad-showd)*

Raemonika *(Pro: ray-mo-nee-kuh)*

I think this name was made famous by the Singing Nun in the 60's, or was that Dominica?

Rankeisha *(Pro: ran-key-shuh)*

Ridgeway *(Pro: rij-wei)*

Sounds like the name of a scenic highway, or a fancy breed of dog.

Ronjella *(Pro: ron-jel-uh)*

Another traumatized Daddy's Little Girl.

Rudale *(Pro: roo-dale)*

Her parents are going to rue the day they came up with this masterpiece.

~ S ~

Sameatria *(Pro: suh-mee-tree-uh)*

Santricia   *(Pro: san-tree-see-uh)*

Senjamin   *(Pro: sen-juh-min)*

Must be related to Benjamese.

Shavella   *(Pro: shuh-vel-uh)*

How about Marvella and Shavella for your twins?

Shawnquetta   *(Pro: shawn-kwet-uh)*

Wow, this name makes a statement! I don't know what kind of statement, but it makes one.

Shelfunda   *(Pro: shel-fun-duh)*

This name is despicable!

Sherdina   *(Pro: shur-ee-nuh)*

Sojourner   *(Pro: soh-jurn-ur)*

Stop laughing!

Spearman   *(Pro: speer-man)*

As in Wrigley spearman gum. What, you didn't know that?

~ T ~

Ta'Tishal   (Pro: ta-tee-shul)

Like I told you, apostophes are the key ingredient to a unique name.

Tamarick   (Pro: tuh-mar-ick)

Tamorse   (Pro: tuh-mor-s)

Named after a former method of communicating in code.

Tangela   (Pro: tan-jel-uh)

Love this name … It's so citrusy!

Tashaleana   (Pro: ta-shuh-lee-on-uh)

Teresita   (Pro: tur-uh-see-tuh)

Terlicia   (Pro: tur-lee-kuh)

Timwanika   (Pro: tim-wah-nee-kuh)

Trakeca   (Pro: tra-kee-say)

Your child would be proud to have this name! Yeah, sure!

~ U ~

As with the Q, we already used up all of the U's. However, I would like to humbly suggest the name "UNJUST" for your consideration.

~ V ~

Vanielle *(Pro: van-yell)*

This is the male version of Danielle. Some of you may have been under the false impression that it was the female version of Daniel. Of course, I'm not sure where Haniel fits in. I'm so confused!

Varnzell *(Pro: varn-zel)*

Vilvelis *(Pro: vil-vel-is)*

Aftershave? Hair gel?

Viteacia *(Pro: vie-tay-see-uh)*

Put a little of this in your morning smoothie and you'll feel good all day.

Varshanika *(Pro: var-shuh-nee-kuh)*

Isn't this something you apply to your wood deck each year?

~ W ~

Waynea   *(Pro: way-nee-uh)*

Female version of Wayne.

Wylema   *(Pro: wahy-lee-muh)*

Waukenia   *(Pro: wau-kee-nee-uh)*

Walhab   *(Pro: wal-hab)*

Clearly, Wally must have been in rehab. Maybe they shouldn't have let him out.

~ Y ~

Yewanda   *(Pro: yuh-wan-duh)*

Poor Wanda keeps getting stuck in the middle of some whacky names.

~ Z ~

Zetwat   *(Pro: ze-twat)*

I get a real charge out of this name!

Zonnarae   *(Pro: zon-uh-ray)*

As in, "I've been exzonerated of all charges".

EPILOGUE

Now that you've read the book, perhaps you would like to join me in thanking all of the parents who decided to indulge themselves when naming their children. I've seen these names a hundred times and I still find myself laughing out loud. I mean, how could you ever get tired of Shitthead, Starshema or Nakedria? I guess some things are just timeless. I don't know about you, but whenever I see the names Famica Dinette or Cleopatria, I'm just so Gladlicia. These and many of the other names are so Wonderful, Marvelous and Unique that they make me feel like the Asa Spades. The Behavior exhibited by these parents has brought so much Anjoylus to my life, especially when I'm having a Ronrico and coke.

Maybe you found some of the names offensive, for example, Placenta. However, it would be a Psin if you felt that way. Perhaps a spin in your Ja'cedes or some Lemonjello would make you feel better? I will tell you this, I have no Tamorse in writing this Poetry Book (Ok, so it's not exactly poetry). I'm certainly not going to get an Ecedric headache over some touchy people who are too Capricious to appreciate my effort. I do know that it would be A Miracle if this book made it on the best seller's list. If it does I'm going to celebrate with some Delisha champagne and take some time off to Delonder my next project. This book has been such a Pashen of mine for so long that I need to Daborleek into other things. Perhaps a trip on the Nautica or becoming a Jazzlyn musician should be my next path. Ah, who am I kidding? I'm a crazy name junky. I love names as much as I love my Mannoris.

In conclusion, I hope that you had a Mighty Fine time in reading my book. Until the next time, good night Aquaneeta, wherever you are!

7607208R0

Made in the USA
Charleston, SC
22 March 2011